CHAGALL
MY SAD AND JOYOUS VILLAGE

CONTENTS

Cover Photo: Chagall, *Me and the Village*

Graphic Design: Sandra Brys, Dominique Mazy (Zig-Zag)

First published in the United States in 1994
by Chelsea House Publishers

© 1989 by Casterman, Tournai

First Printing

1 3 5 7 9 8 6 4 2

ISBN 0-7910-2807-0

ART FOR CHILDREN

CHAGALL

MY SAD AND JOYOUS VILLAGE

By Jacqueline Loumaye

Illustrated by Veronique Boiry

Translated by John Goodman

CHELSEA HOUSE PUBLISHERS

NEW YORK • PHILADELPHIA

THE VILLAGE OF MARVELS

S o, Vitebsk is not your average village?"

"Perhaps not," Nicholas answered me, putting away some of his music.

Nicholas is my friend. He's a violinist. Each time there's a special day at school he plays for us with his colleagues—a flutist and an accordionist. The three of them make up a small ensemble that often enlivens special events in our city and the surrounding area.

"When you grow up, Giles, you'll come with us!" Nicholas promised me. I like music, too. I can already play *Happy Birthday* on the mandolin. I would surely make more progress if my little sister didn't drive me crazy by interrupting all the time.

Nicholas belongs to a family of musicians. His great-grandfather who lived in Russia played the cello. Nicholas has carefully kept his great-grandfather's instrument. "One day I'll have it repaired," he often says.

If you saw his house, you would want to go back there, just like I do. It's full of treasures: souvenirs of Russia, strange objects like the religious image he calls an icon, and paintings. Above the fireplace, there's a portrait of a funny violinist, with his face painted green, playing on the roof of his house. It's snowing in the village, and the church has a curious little steeple, round like an onion!

"Is that your village?" I asked Nicholas the other day.

"No, but it looks like it. It was painted by a great painter who made the town famous."

That's how we started to talk about the painter Marc Chagall. Vitebsk, Nich-

The Violinist (1912–1913)

olas told me, is Chagall's native city—a rather poor city that, with its church and wooden houses, was really more like a village. Little Marc was the eldest of nine children. His father worked in a fish warehouse. His mother ran a grocery shop. One of his uncles was a barber, while another transported animals in a wagon and played the violin.

That was his uncle Neuch, the man in the picture. Above him, someone was flying in the sky.

"Vitebsk doesn't seem like your ordinary village, does it Nicholas?"

But Nicholas didn't answer right away. He was tuning his violin. The strings have to be very tight and then tuned just right.

Nicholas tried out a fragment of melody and then put down his bow.

"So tell me, Nicholas, did this violinist really have a green face?"

"Probably not, but Chagall preferred it that way."

"So he did the same thing as little kids who color lemons red and cherries yellow?"

"Chagall liked to see the world as children see it. According to him, they're the ones who are right."

"That's funny!"

"No! It's serious. He was as amazed by colors as children are. This is what's called having a sense of the marvelous. If it interests you, Giles, I'll lend you a handsome art book until tomorrow."

Nicholas is really nice to me!

In his library, the books go all the way to the ceiling. He has volumes on the history of music and of Russia, of its powerful czars. Have you heard of Ivan the Terrible, Catherine the Great, and Nicolas II? They reigned over Russia until the revolution. Then the country changed its name. It became the Soviet Union.

After the history section, there's another bookcase with novels and poems.

Nicolas II and Alexandra (here in their coronation robes) were the last czars to reign in Russia. Nicolas II was forced to abdicate after the revolution of February 1917. He and the entire imperial family were executed not long after.

Then come the painters, including Marc Chagall, Nicholas' favorite.

Was that because Chagall was Russian like Nicholas? Because he, too, loved the violin?

For both reasons, probably.

I left with a book that was magical! Really! How else explain the people walking on their heads or flying about like birds, upside-down houses, cows under umbrellas, and roosters in the clouds? Some wild things happen in Vitebsk!

When I returned to Nicholas' house the next day, my head was upside-down. I laughed all alone. I wanted to walk on my hands. I moved forward while only looking backwards.

"Oops, sorry!"

"Be careful!" Nicholas said. "If you knock over my musical scores it'll be a disaster!" After helping him clean up the mess, I sat down normally in a chair and waited for him to put down his violin.

"What if we went to Vitebsk during vacation?"

"Vitebsk! It's far away!" Nicholas answered me. "You have to take a plane and a train to get there. And then, Vitebsk is nothing special."

"Don't people walk through the sky like flying reindeer?"

"Oh, you can see that anywhere! All you have to do is look out the window."

Nicholas is teasing me, I thought. He probably wants some quiet so he can get back to work.

Vacation was approaching, and Nicholas and his friends were rehearsing for a concert to be given at the end of the school year. I was to act in one piece— the role of a fly buzzing across the stage. But the musicians for the performance had much more to do! Even so, Nicholas got up and went to get a photo album in the next room.

"You see! That's my great-grandmother Zina, whose husband played the cello. I've already told you about her."

There she was, seated on a small bench with a hen pecking the ground at her feet. Above her a bird flew in the sky. But nobody else was up there.

"Obviously that's not Vitebsk."

The Rooster (1929)

"But it's the same in Vitebsk!" Nicholas assured me. "Unless, all of a sudden, you begin to dream. Then the hen can take great-grandmother Zina on her back and people can fly like birds. Why not?"

"So did Chagall paint while he was asleep?"

"Not at all! He was very much awake, but that didn't stop him from dreaming! He took up his brush, palette, and paints, and represented things as he saw them— his village, his parents, his wife, household objects, his favorite animals, and the small violin that always plays the same tune, the song of the Rabbi of Vitebsk, everywhere in the world.

"For Chagall traveled a great deal and lived a very long time, almost a hundred years! He never stopped painting! And he was always telling his story.

"You see, Giles, this is where he lived. In the Jewish quarter of Vitebsk. The houses are made of wood, and the gardens, enclosed by wooden fences. Everybody spends time in the streets: old and young, beggars and children alike. A real *shtetl!* That's what they call a Jewish village. The carousel turns in the square. Clowns and acrobats move through the town. Occasionally, somebody gets up on a roof for a better view. And from up there you can see the church steeples and the roofs of the synagogues."

This was his village. Sad and joyous at the same time.

"It's just as though one were there!" I said.

"Careful you don't fall!" Nicholas answered, laughing. "You're not used to climbing on roofs!"

"There's no danger. The house doesn't seem very high."

"You know what? Sometimes Marc's grandfather went up on the roof to eat carrots!"

"It's a pretty good painting."

"Do you understand better now what inspired Chagall's imagination?"

"Did the whole family live in a little wooden house?"

"Certainly. When it got dark, Feiga-Ita, Marc's mother, closed up her shop and hurried home. The six little girls and

"Really, how could anyone be born here? How could anyone breathe here?" Chagall asked himself when he visited the tiny house in which he'd been born many years earlier.

In a book entitled *My Life*, which he illustrated using etching and dry point, Chagall told the story of his infancy and childhood.

The Animal Merchant
(1912)

two brothers were already sitting around the table. Soon their father, Sachar, arrived as well. But he was so tired that he asked to go to sleep after the meal, close to the heater. All day he'd been handling little salted herrings in a big barrel. His hands were still frozen, and his clothes were full of salt! Sometimes little uncle Neuch spent the evening with them. He sat on a chair and accompanied Feiga-Ita with his violin. Marc loved to go with him into the country, to look for animals in his wobbly wagon.

"You know," added Nicholas, "Marc's grandmother was a butcher. 'The handsome profession!' the family joked. But that didn't interest Marc at all. He preferred to paint cows, and that also went for his uncle Neuch's horse and donkey. In blue, in red, why not? And also the rooster, and the cat. He was very fond of animals."

"Like me! I love Melon, my black cat that doesn't look like a melon at all!"

THE HOLIDAYS AND THE TRADITIONS

Solitude (1933)

ook closely, Giles," Nicholas said to me, showing me a superb painting. "It must be one or two o'clock in the morning. It's not yet light. Outside the village a rabbi is praying with the Torah in his hands."

"Is that the red scroll?"

"Yes. It contains the laws of the Jewish religion, the ones given to his people by the prophet Moses at Mount Sinai."

"Why is he all alone?"

"Because everyone else is still asleep. But candles are already being lit at the synagogue. It's a feast day. Soon Marc arrives with his family. His father, Sachar, is dressed in white. His mother is going to read a text from the Bible, and she'll shed a tear on the page."

"Is she sad?"

"Not really, but Sachar had told her that was the custom. Marc chants the prayers with others, kneeling. The ceremony is long and he's becoming bored. The door is open.

Chagall's parents belonged to the Jewish sect known as the Hasidim, which stressed prayer over textual study. In his book, Chagall says that the Feast of the Great Pardon made a great impression on him.

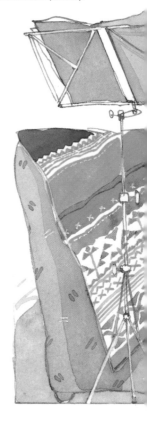

"He slips outside without making a sound."

"And no one sees him?"

"Happily, no! Now he's in the garden. A little cow is chewing its cud under an apple tree. Uncle Neuch has left his violin close by her. A star is giving its last twinkle in the sky. Marc takes a big green apple and bites into it. How delicious! And to think it's forbidden! You're supposed to fast until prayer is over. The ceremony comes to an end. Now everyone can go back to bed."

"Without eating?"

"Of course!" said Nicholas. "But don't worry: there'll be plenty of food at breakfast! Tea and cookies. And herring, pickles, cheese, bread, and butter. The whole family is there, aunts, uncles, and cousins. The samovar is being prepared. There's singing. Uncle Neuch plays the violin. Grandfather listens to him, dreaming. Marc draws at a corner of the table. 'Can I make your portrait, Uncle Israel?' he asks. But his faith forbids it. Unlucky for Marc, who loves to draw!"

Chagall did not adhere to the Jewish tradition that, on the authority of certain passages in the Bible, prohibited the representation of God. "Do not make false gods. . . . Do not prostrate yourselves before sculpted stone . . . for I am the Lord thy God." Likewise, the Jewish religion forbade the representation of men, who are in the image of God. *Leviticus* 26.1

I bet he didn't like school!"

"You're right," said Nicholas. "At the window of his class he looked out at the trees. The only subject that interested him was geometry. He drew lines, triangles, and squares. That he liked!"

"I don't like school very much, either! I much prefer music."

"Marc, too. Before he painted he played the violin. He sang and wrote poems. However, by the time he was eight he knew he would be a painter. What did it matter what the rabbis thought! He made portraits of his sisters, his brother, his parents, his aunts, and above all his little uncle Neuch, of whom he was very fond. In drawing class he was king! One day, walking through the village, he saw a big sign: 'Drawing and Painting School of the Painter Penne.' That's what he needed! Right away Marc went to find his mother. 'Listen, mama, I want to be a painter!' he said to her. 'It's over, I'll never be a warehouse clerk like papa, nor an accountant, nor a butcher!'

Drawings from his youth

" 'A painter? You? You're crazy!' " his mother answered. " 'Let me put my bread in the oven. You're in my way.'

" 'Mama, I insist! Come with me!'

"And in the end Feiga-Ita, his mother, consented. The next day they decided to pay Mr. Penne a visit. But if you could only know, Giles, how disappointed he was!" Nicholas continued. "There was no longer any question of painting his uncle Neuch, his horse and his violin, and objects dear to him, like the clock in the dining room. Imagine him surrounded by plaster casts and silence. It was much

too serious! Would you be interested in the nose of Emperor Caesar Augustus?"

"Not really."

I should say that I'd gotten used to being carried away by Nicholas's stories and I suddenly felt earthbound, for he'd stopped talking about Chagall's early life. The objects around me had settled back into their places. The pendulum clock on the mantle indicated six o'clock. It was time to go home. Nicholas put his violin into its case and left for the evening rehearsal.

I had to wait two days to hear the rest. Nicholas went on tour a hundred miles from here with the trio known as "The Traveling Finches." What a pity I had to go to school and could not go with them! Fortunately, summer was approaching.

I walked past Nicholas's house. He had closed all the shutters. It seemed to me that when he opened them again everything would escape—objects, books, the candleholders on the mantle—and that we might even see a guardian angel on the roof.

We got together again on Friday at four o'clock.

"Not long after we left off," Nicholas said immediately, "our friend Marc left Vitebsk and little Mr. Penne. He managed to get to Saint Petersburg with 27 rubles in his pocket. 'It's all I can give you!' his father had said to him while tending the samovar. 'Do the best you can!' It wasn't very much. And after the trip itself, he had to pay for food and lodging."

"How did he manage?"

"He painted signs for the city's shops. Then he worked for a photographer, which made him a few more rubles. All the while he was attending the city's art school. But it wasn't much better than Mr. Penne's school!"

"Was he still drawing ancient Romans?"

"Romans, vases, still lifes. It didn't suit Chagall at all! It was cold in the classroom and smelled of cabbage. After two years he'd had enough. Then he heard about the school of the painter Bakst, who was beginning to make a name for himself. He decided to introduce himself.

" 'I'm Marc,' he whispered timidly. 'I have an empty stomach and no money, but people say I'm talented.'

Woman with Bouquet (1910)

"Mr. Bakst smiled into his beard. 'We'll give it a try!' he said."

Marc made rapid progress. He discovered the great modern painters Cézanne, Manet, Monet, and Matisse, who were much discussed at Bakst's school. So that was how they painted in Paris! Chagall added bright reds and blues to his palette. His painting took on the celebratory colors that would soon become typical of all his work.

While I did my homework that evening after leaving Nicholas's, I was thinking the whole time about Chagall's courage.

The Algerian Woman, Matisse (1909)

inally, school was over. I got pretty good grades. Me, who's so distracted! Like Chagall, I spend too much class time looking out the window. But now I want to tell you about our performance. It was terrific! The painted sets for "Alice in the Wonderland of Our Own Time" were super. There were sparklers and motorbikes on the stage. The actors wore checkered cardboard costumes, and the music composed by Nicholas's accordionist friend was something else. The whole thing was unforgettable.

"We might have been at the Beehive!" said Nicholas after the performance.

"The Beehive?"

"That's the studio where Marc Chagall settled after arriving in Paris."

"He went to Paris?"

"Why yes! He was able to realize that dream in 1910. Paris, the city of light, fascinated him. And now he was there, along with artists from all over the world. The painters Modigliani and Delaunay became his friends. Poets came to admire his works. Sometimes they were surprised by the objects of all kinds he included in his canvases: clocks, crucifixes, candleholders, animals. 'These are my memories!' Chagall explained. 'They're part of my life and work.' The poet Blaise Cendrars said to him, 'I have the impression it's my own head that's floating through space!' Another poet, Apollinaire, exclaimed, 'This is supernatural painting!' There was no other word for it. Because it was true that Chagall was quickly getting free of contemporary fashion. Cubism? He used it, so long as it didn't prevent him from painting upside-

The Beehive, entrance

The studios

I and the Village (1912)

down figures and topsy-turvy houses! 'Let others eat their square pears at their triangular tables,' said Chagall. 'Myself, it doesn't suit me. I must tell my story in my own way.'

"In his studio he worked night and day, even though no one was buying his paintings. Money was scarce. He would buy half a cucumber and a herring, dividing it in two—eating the head the first day and the tail the next. But that didn't prevent him from being happy!

" 'Paris, you are my second Vitebsk!' he would exclaim."

THE WAR

A nd yet Chagall didn't forget Russia. One day he decided to return, to attend the marriage of one of his sisters and to see Bella.

"Who is Bella?"

"It was still a secret. Chagall had met her in Vitebsk. He'd never forgotten her. Time had passed. Did Bella remember him? Yes! Bella was waiting for him! A few months later they were married. 'I had only to open the window of my bedroom, and blue air, love, and flowers came through it with her!' "

At my house, from the window of my bedroom, I can see a large chestnut tree. In spring it is covered with flowers that resemble candles. One day, while I was writing a piece for school on the "awakening of nature," I counted 125! On just one side!

"Bella was very artistic. She loved Chagall's paintings. He told her about Paris, the Beehive, and his friends. They decided to return together. In the meantime, in 1916, they had a little girl. They named her Ida. But they had to wait before going back to Paris."

"Why?"

"Because war was declared. There was no question of leaving Russia. Chagall was drafted. He, an artist, was going to carry a rifle! Impossible! Finally, he was sent to Saint Petersburg, where he served in a military office until the end of the war."

"So he got through it alright."

"Yes. But at the end of the war, in 1917, revolution broke out!"

"What happened then?"

"In the beginning, Chagall was happy. The czars were gone and the Jews could leave their ghetto. Chagall was asked by the government to found an academy where all forms of art would be represented, even house painting! They decorated residences, tramways, and railroad cars. But why paint green cows and revolutionaries like acrobats, with their feet in the air? That's not serious, comrade Chagall!"

"Was he disappointed?"

"Very much. He began to dream about returning to France."

In October 1917, anarchy prevailed in Russia. A provisional government had replaced that of the czars, but it was confronted with widespread discontent among the workers, who assaulted the Winter Palace in Saint Petersburg, its headquarters.

VITEBSK COMES TO PARIS

iles, do you remember Blaise Cendrars?" Nicholas asked me.

"He's the poet friend of Chagall's."

"Blaise Cendrars wrote to Chagall: 'Come back, here you are famous and people are waiting for you.' That was in 1923. Chagall returned to Paris with Bella, his rooster, his uncle Neuch, his cow and his violin, the angel, the candle-holder, and the church bell tower. It was all of Vitebsk that arrived in Paris!"

"But the big blue shadow is the Eiffel Tower!"

"It's Paris and Vitebsk at the same time! Paris the second Vitebsk, as Chagall had already said."

Here are some lines from a poem by Blaise Cendrars that I copied from one of Nicholas's books:

He sleeps
He's awakened
Suddenly, he paints
He takes a church and paints
with a church
He takes a cow and paints
with a cow
With a sardine

"You know, I've never been to Paris."

"Well, it's summer, so maybe we can think about going. On the same trip I could take my grandfather's cello to be repaired by a musical-instrument maker who's very nice. I'm sure he would put us up."

The Married Couple of the Eiffel Tower (1938)

Blaise Cendrars

"That's great! Can we go tomorrow?"

"For goodness sake, give me time to make the arrangements!"

I was so impatient that I was ready to go right away.

"Can we go to the Beehive?"

"Unfortunately, the studios are destroyed, but we can go to Beaubourg, and we'll see the ceiling of the opera-house painted by Chagall."

At the opera! That would be better than our school performance, or even the circus. I was sure of it!

My parents knew Nicholas well, and they were perfectly willing to leave me in his hands for a few days.

Nicholas thought we might leave on Thursday and return the following Monday.

"Thursday! That's a whole week away! The time will pass very slowly."

"Time knows no bounds!" Nicholas answered me.

And since I didn't understand right away, he added, "That's the title Blaise Cendrars gave to this painting by Chagall. It means that time, on the contrary, passes all too quickly!"

"But this painting's outrageous! A pendulum clock carried through the air by a winged fish playing the violin!"

"When nothing is in its usual place, neither animals nor objects, do you know what that's called, Giles? Surrealism. For the surrealists," Nicholas continued, "the world is not always the way we see it. It can also be as we imagine it, completely different! The brush is unfettered! It makes shapes and invents colors as it goes along. A painter works a bit like an automaton.

"But I," protested Chagall, "belong to no school. What you see is just a dream, nothing more. Perhaps mine, perhaps that of the couple sleeping on the riverbank. I heed nothing but my own fantasy!"

I tried this approach myself. I made a portrait of Nicholas the way I wanted it to be.

"That's me, absolutely," he said laughing.

Finally, the day for our departure arrived.

Time Knows No Bounds
(1938)

Usually, I don't get up so early. But today, thanks to Nicholas, I got up at sunrise. The sky was pink from one end to the other, and the little Peugeot automobile was shining like a carriage in front of the house.

"You haven't forgotten anything?" Nicholas asked me.

I had my toothbrush and my pajamas. I put my bag on the backseat beside the cello, and we were off. The roads were empty. Birds walked on them calmly. In the fields, the cows were still asleep. The horses looked at us as we passed.

"Good day!" I hollered out the window. It seemed to me they shook their manes in response.

"You're not wrong!" said Nicholas. "Chagall, who loved animals, attributed human feelings to them. On his return to Paris, he was very pleased when Ambroise Vollard suggested he illustrate the fables of La Fontaine. Like him, La Fontaine used animals to tell people's stories. Chagall added his own fantasy into the mix. Do you remember the tale of 'The Lion Who'd Gotten Old'? La Fontaine tells the very serious story of an old lion who'd lost all his strength, and was kicked and bitten by all the other animals. Chagall

put a little blue donkey jumping about at the top of the painting, making the story comic instead of tragic!"

When we stopped at noon to picnic in a field, for the first time I wasn't afraid of the cows that were nearby. They seemed nice! Though I did regret that they were only black and white. They're even nicer in red or blue, as Chagall painted them! The flies, on the other hand, were annoying. There was no getting rid of them. We found several drowned in our orange juice, and I said to myself: so much the worse for them!

The Lion Who'd Gotten Old (1926–1927)

We had traveled all day. The weather was superb and the landscape very beautiful.

"You know," Nicholas said to me, "Chagall and his wife traveled all over France: Brittany, the Pyrenees, the Alps, the Mediterranean coast. His palette became lighter and brighter. He painted the countryside, bouquets of flowers, animals, and farm life."

That gave us the idea, when evening came, to ask a farmer if we could sleep in his barn.

"Of course!" the farmer said.

When the farmer saw the cello in the car, he invited us to dinner and asked us to play a little something before going to bed.

"Gladly!" answered Nicholas. "But normally I play the violin."

We emptied the car in the middle of the farmyard. A fine rooster looked at us, perched on one leg. I understand why Chagall loved to paint them.

That evening Nicholas proposed to make blinis. These are delicious little crepes eaten in Russia in the spring. Since there was no caviar, we filled them with cheese. Here's the recipe:

½ lb. of whole wheat flour
¼ lb. of buckwheat flour
2 tablespoons of milk
1 oz. of baker's yeast
3 eggs
3 tablespoons of oil
¼ lb. of melted butter
Mix all the ingredients together and prepare in a hot pan like crepes.

Be forewarned that tossing them in the pan is not easy!

After the meal, Nicholas told the story of his great-grandmother Zina, who had fled from Russia during the revolutionary upheaval. With Nicholas's baby grandfather in her arms, she had crossed the whole of Europe to reach France. Then Nicholas played a gypsy song on his grandfather's cello. And he got through it pretty well, too, because everyone applauded. For a brief moment, this small French village could have been Vitebsk.

It had already been dark for some time when we got back to the barn. The moon shone in the middle of the stars, but not at the same time as the sun, as this jokester Chagall sometimes imagined!

he next morning we were awakened by a strange sound.

"Do you hear that, Nicholas?"

"It's just a cow mooing!" Nicholas sighed, rubbing his eyes.

"No! I think it's an elephant!"

"You're dreaming, Giles."

"Not at all! I was very much awake, and I'm sure."

Then the farmer came to make an announcement: "A circus has come to the village!"

I knew I could tell the difference between a cow and an elephant!

After a bowl of milk and some bread and jam, we headed toward the village. There was much agitation. Trucks, horses, and trailers. Preparations were under way to raise an enormous tent.

"These are people of the road," Nicholas said to me, "nomads who move from town to town with the circus. Chagall, who could remember gypsies and clowns from his childhood in Vitebsk, depicted them in many paintings."

"He liked the circus?"

"He adored it! In Paris he went to the Winter Circus with his friend Vollard all the time. There were very few movie houses at the time, and television hadn't been invented. That's why people went to the theater and the circus more often. The clowns known as Popov and Chocolate were real stars! Chagall painted horseback riders, acrobats, and trapeze artists. The circus was full of magic for him. There people did somersaults, danced, and walked on their hands! Chagall loved its festive side. His color flew

Chagall painting Bella.

The Blue Circus (1950)

from one edge of the canvas to the other, overrunning the contours. As usual he ignored all the rules, including those of perspective. He didn't need them with his magic color, for it circulated and bustled about on its own, creating an impression of movement. Chagall was becoming greater and greater as a colorist."

We'd talked so much about the circus that I wanted to go!

"We could go to the performance tonight!" proposed Nicholas.

I jumped for joy. At eight o'clock we settled in the stands. A drum roll announced the beginning of the performance. Some horses galloped in with a rider doing somersaults on their backs.

A clown juggled a thousand hoops! And when it came time for the trapeze artists, you could have heard a pin drop. For them, as for Chagall, there was no difference between up and down!

BEAUBOURG AND THE MARAIS

Paris through the Window (1913)

aturday morning we were back on the road to Paris. On the outskirts of the city we hit a terrible traffic jam.

"Are you sure where we get off, Giles?

I had a giant map of Paris on my knees.

Porte des Lilas! We'd already passed it! Half an hour later we reached Saint Paul, in the quarter known as the Marais. What quiet! Several shops were closed.

"Many Jews live here," Nicholas explained, "and Saturday is their sabbath, which is to say their day of prayer and rest. Like Sunday for Christians."

We arrived at the musical-instrument maker's house.

"You're finally here!" he exclaimed.

"Come quick! I've prepared a big meal in the kitchen."

We went through his shop, where the ceiling was so low Nicholas could touch it with his finger. Imagine the cave of a music-loving Ali Baba! There were dozens of violas and violins hanging from the rafters. There were also three mandolins, five cellos, and two double-basses leaning against the wall. In back was another room that served as a workshop. Here Nicholas presented the cello for assessment.

"It isn't serious," the craftsman said quickly. "I'll start on it today."

There were wooden chips scattered everywhere.

"A violin is made up of 85 pieces," he explained. "The last one to be slipped inside the instrument is called its soul. After that it's ready to sing!"

"I'm not surprised that a violin has a soul, because it sometimes makes us laugh and cry. My mandolin, too."

"You play the mandolin?" our host asked.

"I'm just beginning to study."

He lent me an instrument. During the dessert I played *Claire de Lune* without a single mistake!

"And now we'd better be off," said Nicholas, "if we want to get to Beaubourg this afternoon."

"That's easy," the musical-instrument maker explained. "You get on the metro at the Saint-Antoine stop and get off at Rambuteau."

In the Marais quarter in Paris, there are many shops selling Jewish specialties.

There was a crowd in the square when we arrived, as though some sort of celebration were being prepared. I gave my hand to Nicholas so I wouldn't get lost. In front of us rose the mass of big pipes and girders that is the Georges Pompidou National Center of Art and Culture, or Beaubourg for short. Some people said

the building resembled a factory, but I thought it was a success. And the proof was that everyone here seemed to be having such a great time. One had only to see the people circled around the fire-eaters, musicians, and dancers to know this.

How Chagall would have loved to paint this vision in the bright afternoon sun! If Nicholas had brought his violin, he'd have been able to play like uncle Neuch, who livened things up on special occasions. He would certainly have been a success, and we'd have earned some money to pay for the cello repairs!

"I must confess I hadn't thought of that," said Nicholas, pulling me toward the museum.

There was a long line at the entrance. It was not moving, so I sat down for five minutes on a step and took out my drawing pad.

What if I tried to draw a juggler? The problem is he doesn't stop moving! Since it wasn't possible to copy, I had to follow Chagall's example and invent.

"That's not bad!" said Nicholas. "But come back, the line's moving forward."

A few moments later we were in the big entrance hall. On the ground floor there were already a library, a video library, and exhibition spaces. To the right on entering, there was even a studio for children. If I lived in Paris, I could learn to draw there.

"Don't get distracted, Giles. Look where you're going."

We went up an escalator to the fifth floor. Beyond the windows Paris seemed very small, like from an airplane. The Eiffel Tower was visible in the distance. Nicholas promised to take me there.

Fortunately there was a plan at the entrance to the floor, for how were we going to find Chagall among all these other painters?

"Here!" I cried. I recognized it right away. There was a red cow on a roof, and the Vitebsk bell tower.

"This is an important painting," Nicholas explained to me. "The first big work by Chagall after he settled in the Beehive. First he painted the woman farmer going to milk the cow. A familiar scene of country life. Suddenly his brush started to transform everything. Shooting stars illuminate the night. The woman's head floats free in the sky. Look at her dress. With its geometric elements she's fashionably cubist. But she still wears her wooden shoes!"

"The cow is also fashionably square and triangular."

"Yes! But its little tail in the air is full of fantasy."

"And again, everyone's on the roof!"

"Do you see the little calf and the green child, Giles? They recall the old Roman legend of Romulus and Remus being nourished by a she-wolf."

Even so, everything seemed very Russian. In the left corner, Chagall even painted the bucket in which he'd bathed in Vitebsk!

To Russia, Donkeys, and Others (1911)

Before Nicholas had finished speaking I had found another painting.

It would have been hard to miss! It is as though you are in Chagall's house. Bella is there. Around her one can make out the winged pendulum clock, a bouquet, uncle Neuch with his violin, the angel, and the rooster. Myself, I was particularly taken with the little blue cow with an illuminated candelabrum above the houses of Vitebsk.

"Blue and red are the colors that dominate in this painting," Nicholas observed, "as well as in many of his subsequent works."

At the moment, only these two paintings by Chagall were on exhibit. A guard told us there were others in storage.

On our way out of the room, we passed some canvases by Chagall's friend Delaunay, whose handling of color he much admired. Then came Kandinsky, another Russian, and Picasso and Matisse. They had all lived at the same time.

"That's enough for today, don't you think?" asked Nicholas.

It's true that my legs were getting tired; I sure wasn't going to fly away

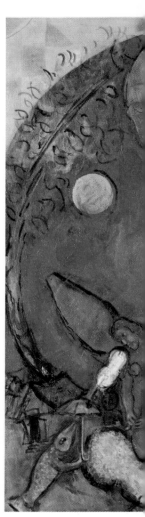

To My Wife (1944)

**With a Black Arc,
Kandinsky**

anytime soon! Except on the escalator, which brought us directly to "seventh heaven!" By that, I mean the top floor of the museum, from which you can see all of Paris.

We went into the restaurant and had some apple pie and lemonade. Around us, birds were flying about looking for crumbs.

"How did they get in here?" Nicholas asked himself.

Perhaps the birds were asking themselves how we managed to get as high up as they are!

Immediately after breakfast, we went out with the musical-instrument maker to explore the Marais.

"I'll do my grocery shopping at the same time," he said.

"Grocery shopping? On Sunday?"

"In the Jewish quarter of the Marais, all the shops are open Sundays; for them it's a normal business day."

First we crossed the Place des Vosges, with its rows of identical houses around a park where children were playing. Then we arrived at the beautiful garden of the Sully Hotel. It was as quiet as a cloister. There are at least a dozen such hotels, or old mansions, in the Marais; one of them, the Salé Hotel, is now the Picasso Museum.

"Perhaps one day Chagall will have his own museum in Paris," I said.

"In the meantime," answered Nicholas, "there's a very beautiful museum devoted to him in Nice. I'll tell you about it later. But now we're in Paris, and there's much to see."

We headed toward Rosiers Street, for time was passing and our host had not yet done his shopping.

Parisians must really love this neighborhood, for along the way we noticed lots of buildings being restored. You can't

The Marais is an old quarter of Paris. In the Middle Ages it was nothing but a marsh until it was dried out by monks. It was in the 17th century, under Henry IV, that the Marais became an elegant neighborhood. Today it still contains many 17th- and 18th-century residences.

imagine the pretty courtyards behind some of the doors!

We arrived at Rosiers Street. What activity! There were lots of rabbis in the street—young ones and old ones.

"No!" Nicholas exclaimed. "The young ones aren't rabbis but Jewish children wearing yarmulkes, or skull-caps, on their heads.

There were no wooden houses, but it still felt like we were walking through Vitebsk, Chagall's old neighborhood.

Noah Releasing the Dove
(1931), Nice

We stopped in front of the window of a Jewish bookstore. I recognized the seven-branched candleholder beside an illustrated Old Testament for children.

"You know," said Nicholas, "Ambroise Vollard also commissioned Chagall to do a set of illustrations for the Bible."

"After the fables of La Fontaine?"

"Yes. That suited Chagall perfectly, for he'd still be able to tell the kind of marvelous stories he loved."

"He went with Bella to Palestine, where he found lots of rabbis and an atmosphere like that of his childhood. It made him so happy that he decided then and there to consecrate his art to the story of the Bible."

We arrived at a very handsome store on a corner.

"This is where we're going," said our host.

The food for sale was unfamiliar. There was gefilte fish, smoked salmon, and other strange things to eat.

Nicholas bought the dessert: a big piece of vatrouchka, a Russian lemon cake.

"I forgot the pickles!" said Nicholas's friend as we were leaving. "That's alright, we can get them at the spice shop we pass on the way."

That place really made you feel like you'd left Paris and were inside Feiga-Ita's shop! The floor was covered with sacks full of dried apricots, pistachios, and, of course, pickles in all shapes and sizes. And there were all kinds of breads: onion, poppy-seed, cumin, sesame-seed —and containers full of salted herring!

We filled our shopping bags. We were loaded up like donkeys and were glad to get home.

"With all this food I can make you a lunch worthy of Vitebsk!"

It was delicious, especially the cake.

THE OPERA

By the time we had taken the metro to the opera it was four o'clock. At four-thirty they stop selling tickets for tours of the building.

"Hurry up!" said Nicholas, running up the grand staircase.

We entered the theater. Above our heads was a huge, brightly colored carousel with a chandelier in the middle. There were dancers, Paris, angelic musicians—and then nothing. The lights went out.

"Nicholas! Where are you?"

The hall had been plunged into darkness. On the stage, under dim light, stagehands were moving ladders and installing the sets for the evening performance. I found Nicholas again on the grand staircase.

The ceiling of the Paris Opera

I felt as sad as though I had arrived at a celebration too late, after it was all over.

"Take heart!" said Nicholas. "I have another idea. We'll try and get tickets for tonight's performance."

At the ticket window the program was listed: *The Magic Flute* by Mozart.

"What luck!" added Nicholas. "We may be able to see an opera for which Chagall designed the sets in 1967!"

We had to come back an hour before the curtain. Finally, after a long wait in line, we found ourselves at the top of the theater.

Fortunately our host had lent us his opera glasses, for we sure needed them! On the other hand, we were very close to the ceiling, which we could see perfectly.

On the stage the red curtain was still lowered. But up here, in paradise, the music had already started!

"Chagall was 77 when he undertook this demanding work," Nicholas told me. "Look at the whirlwind of colors! Green for Wagner and Berlioz. White for Rameau and Debussy. Red for Ravel and Stravinsky. Yellow for Tchaikovsky. Blue for Mussorgsky; he's painted as an icon! Blue also for Mozart; it's *The Magic Flute*, which we're seeing tonight."

We had time to recognize a bird, a violin, a flute, and a fish in the middle of dancers and angels in the sky.

Then the chandelier went out, and the curtain rose on the performance.

Chagall's angel lent his golden flute to Prince Pamino to charm the wild animals, who went to sleep at his feet. Papagéno answered with his pipes. He captured the birds for the Queen of the Night, who had a voice as high as a lark in the sky!

Did the music rise from the stage or come down from the ceiling? It was so captivating that it seemed to animate the figures above our heads. The dancers were set dancing, the birds chirping, and uncle Neuch disguised himself so he could play his violin with the angels!

I didn't know whether to look up or down, and I wanted to sing myself!

"Don't move about so much," whispered Nicholas. "You'll fall!" Everyone applauded. The performance was over. The chandelier lit up again, and it was as though the sun had risen in the sky where Chagall's figures were floating.

André Malraux was a close friend of Chagall's. When he was French Minister of Cultural Affairs, he commissioned Chagall to paint the ceiling of the Paris Opera.

Memories of the Magic Flute (1976)

The next morning we returned to the Place des Vosges. It is more or less the neighborhood garden, and it is very pleasant there. We passed in front of Victor Hugo's house and the one in which Madame de Sévigné, the famous French letter-writer, was born. Then we sat down on a bench, and Nicholas told me how Chagall's life had not been all roses.

"Many sad things happened to him, most seriously the death of Bella in 1944 in the United States."

"He had left France?"

"Chagall was compelled to leave because of the Nazi atrocities against the Jews. Fortunately, the Museum of Modern Art in New York invited him to seek refuge there. So he set out for the United

War (1943)

States with Bella and his daughter Ida in 1941. That same day, Adolf Hitler invaded Russia. Chagall was very disturbed by this. In his distress he painted several works on the theme of war. Three years later, in 1944, Bella suddenly fell ill and died in the hospital. It took Chagall an entire year to recover from her death. This master of color explained that everything had become black for him, and that it was impossible for him to paint.

"Like in the sky over our heads."

A large cloud had obscured the sun, turning everything gray.

"Don't be sad, Giles. Chagall found happiness again."

"How did it happen?"

"It was thanks to Vava. On leaving the United States, Chagall settled in the south of France, in Provence. It was there that one day he met Valentine Brodsky. She was very tender with him and restored all his energy, all his taste for life and color. Despite his age, Chagall would still undertake demanding works like the ceiling we just saw at the Paris Opera. Soon he realized a long-standing dream to paint scenes from the Bible. These works are all in Nice, in the Museum of the Biblical Message. They convey what Chagall felt to be most important: that we should all strive to make peace and joy prevail in the world."

Then Nicholas showed me one of Chagall's portraits of Vava. She had a green face, like the violinist on the roof! To signify his love for her, Chagall painted a pair of lovers on her dress and a fine red horse beside her.

German troops invading Russia in 1941.

A SUNLIT PARADISE

O n a whim, we decided to go to Nice instead of staying in Paris. I must admit that we were drawn there as much by the sun as by Chagall.

"What a great idea it was to come here!" said Nicholas. "There are so many beautiful paintings here. It's really a festival of light."

I saw blue, red, and green. One could not help but be joyous there. Our long trip had definitely been worthwhile.

Do you know the story of the Bible? So much the better. But for those who have forgotten some of it, Chagall tells it as though it were his own story, that of his village and his family, with animals in the sky or accompanied by biblical prophets and kings.

I recognized Noah releasing the dove after the flood.

"This one is King David, and that one over there is Abraham," Nicholas explained.

And then there was Adam and Eve in the middle of the earthly paradise. We came to a smaller room with eight sides where there were five paintings in various shades of red. Nicholas thought this was the most beautiful place in the museum.

At the entrance there was a small inscription that read: "To Vava, my wife, my joy, and my happiness."

Nicholas and I quickly agreed about our favorite painting. It represented a marriage inspired by the book of the Bible called "The Song of Songs" (the song of those who love one another).

Why this particular painting? Because

it had Vitebsk and its bell tower upside-down, and all our friends! Bella and Vava, the rabbi with his cane, a bird, and a little donkey wearing a crown because paradise is an unending celebration. Way up in the sky there is an angel lighting candles.

"Look Nicholas, this upside-down Vitebsk doesn't resemble Paris at all."

"That's right. It's Saint-Paul-de-Vence, quite nearby, where Chagall lived with Vava, whom he married in 1952."

But Chagall, who's in a corner with his palette, never forgot the little Russian village of his past, even though he settled in a small French village flooded with sunlight.

The Song of Songs III (1960)

I moved closer to the painting and saw a circus clown, a little goat, a crescent moon, a tree, and a bouquet of flowers. At that point a guard came toward us and explained that Chagall often used a bit of sand to obtain relief effects in his canvases. When you looked at this one from the side you could see he was right.

The guards here did not seem bored or sleepy in their chairs. On the contrary, they offered museum visitors a warm welcome.

"Don't forget the room in the back!" one of them said to us.

This room had two stained-glass windows by Chagall that cast a blue light over everything. They represented the creation of the world.

Stained-glass window in Metz Cathedral

"Chagall was interested in every medium and technique," Nicholas explained. "He was both artist and craftsman. To learn the art of stained glass, he took lessons from a master of the craft. He made his first windows for a little church in the mountains, in Haute-Savoie. That same year he received another commission from Metz Cathedral. Many others would follow."

We sat down a moment to take in the play of light through the windows.

"Have you noticed that it's also a recital hall?" Nicholas asked me.

Indeed, on a platform were a grand piano and a harpsichord decorated by Chagall. Perhaps Nicholas would be invited to play the violin there.

Before leaving, we took time to admire an immense mosaic, in the middle of which was the prophet Elijah in his chariot.

"Old age doesn't dim the creative impulse!" concluded Nicholas. "Chagall was over 60 years old when he learned the art of stained glass, and also those of mosaics and sculpture!"

The First Four Days of Creation, in Nice. The museum is a haven of peace. Visiting it one day, Chagall exclaimed, "God is here."

On our way out we met a group of children younger than I who, after visiting the museum, were taking in the garden with their teacher.

"May we join you?" asked Nicholas, who loved flowers.

"Certainly!" answered the teacher. "The curator herself is about to tell us all about her garden."

Nicholas was very much surprised to see a curator spending time with children. Myself, I thought Chagall would have approved. He loved children so much he wanted to remain one forever!

We started our tour of the garden, and we recognized lavender, thyme, and rosemary.

"Here we have hydrangeas. And there are some more. All these flowers are white and blue like the sky!"

Nicholas wrote down the names in his notebook so he could plant them in his garden in the spring.

The children were happy, laughing and amusing themselves. But they wanted to pick some flowers for bouquets.

After a moment's reflection, the curator made a special exception for them.

Together, she and the teacher composed a little marriage bouquet in the style of Chagall, to honor the fact that we were in his museum and his garden. I like flowers, too, but I like clowns, donkeys, and prophets even more!

Then it was really time to go.

I sent home a postcard from Nice, and Nicholas sent a reproduction of *Paradise*

A poster by Chagall

to his musician friends so they would not think he had forgotten them.

The return trip took two days because we were in no hurry to get back.

The weather was so beautiful that one night we slept under the open sky.

Myself, I was convinced it would stay sunny until the end of the summer.

GLOSSARY

Beauborg: another name for the Pompidou Center, a colorful cultural center in the center of Paris housing the French National Museum of Modern Art.

cubism: style of early–20th-century painting made popular by Pablo Picasso and Georges Braque in which objects are shown from several directions at once.

The Marais is also known for its Jewish restaurants and delicatessens.

Paris' Jewish quarter, the Marais district, is known for its quiet streets and rows of elegant townhouses.

Eiffel Tower: Completed in 1889, this 984-foot-high landmark is the tallest edifice in Paris and one of the most beautiful cast-iron structures in the world.

Elijah: Ninth-century Jewish prophet who defended the God of Israel against the prophets of Baal; according to the Bible, Elijah never died, but rode in a fiery chariot to meet with God in heaven.

The Picasso Museum in the Marais district contains the largest collection of works by Chagall's most famous contemporary.

King David: greatest biblical king of Israel; slayer of the giant Goliath and composer of many of the biblical Psalms.

Marais, the: neighborhood in central Paris known for its quaint streets and elegant town houses.

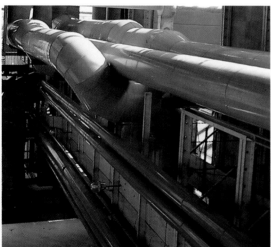

Moses: great bibilical hero who led the Jewish people out of slavery in Egypt and received the Ten Commandments from God on Mt. Sinai.

Mozart, Wolfgang Amadeus (1756–1791): Austrian composer whose operas, *Don Giovanni and the Magic Flute*, are among the greatest achievements in Western music.

rabbi: Jewish religious leader.

Romulus and Remus: mythical twin brothers who were raised by wolves; according to legend, Romulus murdered his brother Remus and later founded ancient Rome.

synagogue: traditional place of worship in the Jewish religion.

The Georges Pompidou Center houses the Museum of Modern Art.

The Museum of Art and Popular Tradition in Nice contains a number of Chagall's paintings.

Chronology

1887	Marc Chagall is born in Vitebsk, Russia
1908	Becomes a student at the Swanseva School, directed by Bakst
1910	Leaves Russia for Paris
1912	Moves into a studio in the Beehive
	Paints his first great works: *To Russia, Donkeys, and Others*; *I and the Village*; *Homage to Apollinaire*
1914	Returns to Vitebsk for a brief visit, but when war breaks out is obliged to remain
1915	Marries Bella Rosenfeld in Vitebsk
1916	Birth of his daughter, Ida
1918	Appointed Commissioner of Fine Arts in Vitebsk and becomes director of the art school there; after a disagreement with Malevitch, another great painter of the time, Chagall resigns
1922	Leaves Russia and settles in Berlin
1923	Ambroise Vollard, a great French dealer, seeks him out; Blaise Cendrars suggests he return to Paris. Illustrates Gogol's *Dead Souls* for Vollard
1926	Illustrates, again for Vollard, the *Fables* of La Fontaine; they would not be published until 1952, by Tériade
1927	Executes gouaches on the theme of the circus for the same patron

1930	Illustrates the Bible
1931	Visits Tel Aviv with his wife and daughter, and works there for a time; publishes *My Life* with Stock
1941	Is invited to seek refuge in New York
1944	Death of Bella
1948	Final return to France
1952	Marries Valentina Brodsky
1955	Begins set of paintings called *The Message of the Bible*
1957	Completes his first mosaic
1958	Creates models for the windows of Metz Cathedral
1963	Begins work on the ceiling of the Paris Opera
1969	Poses the foundation stone of the museum in Nice
1972	Completes the windows for the museum in Nice
To	Numerous exhibitions all over the world; travels widely
1984	Increasingly recognized as one of the great artists of the 20th century; awarded the French Legion of Honor and named honorary citizen of Jerusalem
1985	Dies in Saint-Paul-de-Vence

Where are the paintings by Marc Chagall?

Photographic Credits

For all reproductions of works by Marc Chagall:
© Sabam Brussels
Cover and p. 21 left: Belgian Royal Fine Arts Museums, Brussels/Speltdorn
p. 7: Giraudon
p. 9: Roger-Viollet
p. 11: Scala
p. 13: Migeat/Musée National d'Art Moderne, Paris
p. 14: Tel Aviv Museum
p. 18: Lauros-Giraudon
p. 19: C.F.L. Giraudon
p. 20, left: Roger-Viollet
p. 20, right: Roger-Viollet
p. 21, right: Dorsey/Sipa Icono
p. 23: Harenberg Kommunikation
p. 25, top: R. Rolland/Artephot
p. 25, right: Roger-Viollet
p. 27: Museum of Modern Art, New York
p. 29: Harari Collection
p. 32: Dorsey/Sipa Icono
p. 33: F. Faillet/Artephot
p. 34: Roger-Viollet
p. 39: Musée National d'Art Moderne, Paris
p. 40: Musée National d'Art Moderne, Paris
p. 41: Giraudon
p. 44: Reunion des Musées Nationaux, Paris
p. 49, bottom: Scala
p. 49, right: G. Giribaldi-Gamma
p. 50: Musée National d'Art Moderne, Paris
p. 51: E.R.L./Sipa Icono
p. 53: Réunion des Musées Nationaux, Paris
p. 55: Lauros-Giraudon
p. 55, bottom: Gamma
p. 60, top: Sipa Press
p. 60, lower right: Gamma-Ch. Vioujard
p. 60, lower left: Dorsey/Sipa Press
p. 61: Nisberg/Sipa Press
p. 61, upper right: J.R. Florent/Gamma
p. 61, lower right: Gamma
Most of the information concerning Chagall's youth comes from his book *My Life* (French edition, *Ma Vie*, published by Stock)